SHOW AND TELL

Anthony Clarvoe

BROADWAY PLAY PUBLISHING INC
New York
BroadwayPlayPub.com

SHOW AND TELL
© Copyright 1996 Anthony Clarvoe

The play was first published in January 1996 in the collection *Plays By Anthony Clarvoe*

Cover art direction: Miky Wolf; graphic design: Robert Jansen

First printing August 2020
I S B N: 978-0-88145-877-0

Book design: Marie Donovan
Page make-up: Adobe Indesign
Typeface: Palatino

SHOW AND TELL was commissioned by South Coast Repertory. It was presented by South Coast Repertory as a workshop directed by Lisa Peterson; in the Playwrights' Center's 1991 Midwest Playlabs as a workshop directed by William Partlan; and in readings by Upstart Stage, the Playwrights' Center, and New Dramatists.

The world premiere of SHOW AND TELL was presented on 6 November 1992 by the Repertory Theatre of Saint Louis, Steven Woolf, Artistic Director, Mark D Bernstein, Managing Director. The company was:

COREY	Susan Erickson
SETH	Jim Abele
IRIS/LUCY	Mickey Hartnett
ANN/GAIL	Kim Sebastian
SHARON/ERINN	Brenda Denmark
FARSTED	R Ward Duffy
Director	Susan Gregg
Set and lights	Max De Volder
Costumes	J Bruce Summers
Music and sound	Stephen Burns Kessler
Stage manager	Champe Leary

ACKNOWLEDGMENTS

In addition to those named above, I am especially indebted to David Emmes, Martin Benson, Jerry Patch, and John Glore at South Coast Repertory; Dennis Barnett, Carter Lewis, and Julian López-Morillas at Upstart Stage; David Moore and Jeffrey Hatcher at the Playwrights' Center; and Anne Bogart at New Dramatists for their help with SHOW AND TELL.

My thanks also to the National Endowment for the Arts, the Jerome Foundation, and the Playwrights' Center for their generous financial support during the writing of the script.

CHARACTERS & SETTING

COREY, *early thirties, a schoolteacher*
SETH, *late thirties, a government man*
FARSTED, *late twenties, a working man*
IRIS, *fifties, a coroner*
LUCY, *fifties, a grandmother*
SHARON, *forties, a forensic investigator*
ERINN, *forties, a mother*
ANN, *twenties, an administrative assistant*
GAIL, *twenties, a mother*

IRIS *doubles with* LUCY, SHARON *with* ERINN, ANN *with* GAIL. *These three women are a presence on the stage during some scenes in which their characters do not appear, as noted.*

A wooden institutional table and four wooden chairs. An open space. A door through which the entrances are made.

ACT ONE

Scene One

(COREY *stands downstage. She holds some postcards. There is a soft hissing sound.*)

COREY: In Show and Tell, we find an object we can learn from. We learn who it belongs to and how they use it. Always remember to ask for permission before you bring anything in. (*Three quiet knocks, as if on a door*) Some objects are toys, or tools. The ones I've brought today are souvenirs. A souvenir is a tool for your memory. (*Three quiet knocks*) These are pictures I brought back from a trip I took a long time ago. I'll pass them around in a minute. They're pictures of the capital city. Who can tell us the name of the capital city? That's right. (*She looks at a postcard.*) Here's what the city looks like when you're flying through the air. See all the big white buildings? (*She looks at a postcard.*) This is the Capitol building at night. See the dome on top, all lit up? At night in the city, the lights are so shiny they drown out the stars. The sky is as dark as the land is here. But the streets are so bright, you feel like you're walking through the starry sky. (*She looks at a postcard.*) This is my favorite building: the art museum. The museum is filled with rooms, and every single room is filled with pictures. Do you want to paint pictures later today? Good. (*She looks at a picture in a little frame.*) The last one is a picture that I bought in the museum. It's a picture of a real picture in another

museum, and it's really spooky, see, there's a knight
on a beautiful horse, and his little dog, and the knight
is talking to a skeleton. Some pictures are of animals
or people or nature scenes. This is a picture of an idea.
(*Three quiet knocks*) Those are my objects. You can learn
so much about people by sharing their possessions.
We share them and it's like sharing the people we
care about. (*Three quiet knocks*) We show that we care
by learning. (*Three quiet knocks*) That's what we do in
Show and Tell.

(*Four louder knocks. Lights down on* COREY.)

Scene Two

(SETH *is standing contemplating a spot on the fourth wall at
slightly above eye height.*)

SETH: Iris.

IRIS: What is it, Seth?

SETH: Look at this.

IRIS: What?

SETH: Clear through the wall.

IRIS: It's not—

SETH: Look.

IRIS: Tibia?

SETH: Femur, my guess. Children, remember.

IRIS: Terrible.

SETH: Senseless tragedy. But clear through the wall!
Physics, boy... Bring the staff in, show them this. Why
did no one see this before?

IRIS: We didn't think to look. Clear through—

SETH: When everyone has seen it, get it downstairs with the rest.

IRIS: It's a mess down there. I think we may be looking at a mass grave situation.

(ANN *enters.*)

ANN: Seth? Excuse me? Someone named Sharon says—

IRIS: Sharon's on this one?

ANN: She says—she has arrived and would like to see you.

SETH: Is she on the phone?

(SHARON *enters.*)

SHARON: Live! Live and in person! The message I gave this girl was to tell you to open that door or I'd blow your house in! Gimme some!

(SHARON *throws her arms around* SETH.)

SETH: How about this. Together again.

SHARON: Iris! I see you over there. Keeping an eye on this boy?

IRIS: Sharon. Good to see you.

(*Everyone sits around the table.*)

SETH: Are we up to speed? Sharon?

SHARON: I just got here. I've got a fairly reliable list of the victims, I've had a glance at the physical evidence, I've done a little interviewing. This, forgive me, is one pathetic bunch of survivors. It's time to ask: Is it my imagination or is grief always very tiresome?

IRIS: Never lose your curiosity.

SHARON: I've got it in storage somewhere.

SETH: Good work. Ann?

ANN: We've taken over the school building. The local authorities have the east wing as a communications center. We've pushed the press in there as well.

SETH: Good. They can keep each other company and we'll get our work done. Ann, this is your particular brief. I'll update the press mornings and afternoons, and immediately upon breakthroughs. In exchange, everybody stays where they've been put. Clear?

ANN: Clear.

SETH: People, about the press. Close-order drill. No exclusives, no leaked photographs, and no swarming over the bereaved. All statements coordinated through me. "The governor has committed every resource to ascertaining causes and releasing remains as quickly as possible. We have excellent cooperation from local law enforcement. No one has claimed responsibility, we're ruling nothing out." Ann?

ANN: We put the parents in the west wing. Some are under sedation and we have a room and local medics for them.

SETH: How many grief counselors do we have?

ANN: Ah. Well. There was a carload of them coming up from the city, but their car slid off the road.

SHARON: I love it! The ambulance chases them for a change!

ANN: They're being examined and treated.

SETH: And are helping each other work through the experience, no doubt. Let people know we'll have to take up the slack there for a while.

ANN: There's a room set up for Sharon's forensic work. Iris and the assistant coroners have the victims in the basement.

SETH: Where are the witnesses?

ANN: There were no witnesses per se, everyone in the room was killed.

SHARON: Their teacher was just outside. She was the first one in.

SETH: Where is she?

ANN: I don't know. I've been handling things here.

SHARON: I think I've seen her a couple of places.

SETH: What is she, wandering from room to room? How is she?

SHARON: We got a basic statement....

SETH: Ann, have her found and put her somewhere. Good work.

(ANN exits.)

SETH: Iris?

IRIS: It's a jigsaw puzzle down there. Very few edge pieces.

SHARON: Oy oy oy. Mass grave?

SETH: No. I don't think a mass grave will suffice.

IRIS: Are you asking me to sew name tags onto all of them?

SHARON: Seth! Show everyone a little mercy, huh?

IRIS: You know how much time that would take? I could lose myself in a problem like this for weeks.

SHARON: Weeks? Jesus.

IRIS: You know how I get, down there in the cold rooms.

SETH: I will not tell the peasantry we think of their dead children as an undifferentiated mass. It sends a bad message.

SHARON: Think of what it'll put the families through. They'll start asking themselves why their children are so hard to recognize. They'll try not to picture it, but they will.

SETH: And if we give them a mass grave? What'll they picture then? Their children asleep in each others' arms?

(FARSTED *enters with* ANN *close behind.*)

FARSTED: Excuse me.

ANN: Mr Farsted. If you could just wait out—

FARSTED: Sir?

IRIS: Ann? Who is this?

ANN: I'tem sorry. His son—

IRIS: One of the—?

FARSTED: I'm looking for my boy.

ANN: Didn't the sheriff's office sit everyone down this morning?

FARSTED: I had work. I just need to know what—

ANN: There's a room where you can wait—

FARSTED: I'm looking for the room where I can get my boy and go home. Where's that room at?

SHARON: Mister—

FARSTED: Farsted, Ma'am.

SHARON: Mister Farsted, some people behave as if grief gave them license to act badly. You're not like that, are you?

FARSTED: But—

ANN: Mister Farsted, if you'd come with me—

FARSTED: Don't I have a right to get my son back? If I have to sign something, I'll sign. I can prove he's mine. I know the government has its own way of doing things. If I need to pay someone, for a permit, a little compensation for your trouble, I'll do it. Name your price. My wife—

SETH: Where is your wife?

FARSTED: They have her in a room where she has to lie down.

SETH: Mister Farsted. First of all, let me express that I cannot possibly feel the depth of your loss. Secondly, I am speaking to you with the utmost frankness. I expect you to be discreet with what I tell you.

FARSTED: Thank you, sir.

SETH: You needn't call me sir. Were you in the service?

FARSTED: In peacetime.

SETH: Nonetheless, you know what an explosion can do. If I tell you there was a massive explosion at very close quarters, you know what that means.

FARSTED: They're hard to identify. The bodies.

IRIS: If it were even that simple.

SHARON: You have to understand: When death comes like this it leaves almost nothing intact.

SETH: That's how we know they died instantly.

FARSTED: Really?

SETH: No question. Now looking at your son and the other children will help us learn the cause.

FARSTED: His momma keeps asking for him.

SETH: Mister Farsted, what made him your son is not downstairs.

FARSTED: I want what's left. A box with his name on it, anything at all, she keeps asking and asking and somebody has to stop her, I can't make her stop, I can't force her to, I mean you'd have to be an animal.

SETH: We shall identify the dead, and we shall place the blame. We have been sent here to name the names, and we shall not rest until we do. Will that satisfy you?

FARSTED: Yes, sir. Thank you, sir.

ANN: This way, Mr Farsted.

(ANN *shows* FARSTED *out and is about to follow.*)

SETH: Ann. In the future, have the door more carefully watched. Please.

ANN: Yes, Seth. I'm very sorry. (*She exits.*)

IRIS: Merciful God.

SHARON: Aren't you happy in your job, Seth? Don't you welcome each new day?

IRIS: Are you willing to endure weeks of that?

SETH: If we leave them a mass grave, they'll have to endure it forever. You heard the man. They need something with the name of what they loved.

IRIS: They will not get what they loved. What they will get, if they insist on getting something, will be a few human parts, inevitably mixed with a certain amount of desk and textbook and so on.

SETH: Give them anything they can bury.

IRIS: I will not misidentify remains.

SHARON: You're both right, okay? You're both too fair for this world, okay? Now. Iris, start piecing them together. Don't worry about the names yet. Seth promised, you gonna make a liar out of him? Huh?

IRIS: All right.

SHARON: You're a champ. Seth, people care about you. Take it into account. Now make a statement. Don't say they're unidentifiable. Say we need the remains for the investigation. When they start screaming, blame it on me.

SETH: Sharon, I couldn't ask you to—

IRIS: I'll try and see that it doesn't come to that.

SHARON: Christ, the time you people waste being right.

IRIS: Off we go. (*She exits.*)

SHARON: Already we've got a fight. You're not making this any easier.

SETH: It's not supposed to be easy.

SHARON: Can I give you some advice? An event this bad, you bundle it up neat and you get the hell away. I'm doing my job, okay? But I am nothing here but cameras and tweezers and little plastic bags.

SETH: Have I asked for anything else?

SHARON: From me? No. From you, I don't know.

SETH: I'm just working.

SHARON: Good, because if you start feeling this one, kiddo, you will be gone gone gone. You hear me?

SETH: I hear you.

SHARON: Good. Now come on, let's go wading.

(SHARON *exits.* SETH *looks at the bone in the wall as the lights fade.*)

Scene Three

(Corey stands holding an autoharp case. There are splatters of blood on her arms. GAIL is sitting at the table with her head down, sedated. Suddenly, as if a door had been opened onto the sound, a woman wails and sobs, "No, no, no, no," and is subdued. LUCY enters, carrying a shopping bag full of child's art. She turns back to call:)

LUCY: Erinn! This must be the place!

(LUCY sits near GAIL as ERINN enters.)

LUCY: Gail, here you are, darling. Right, you just rest.

ERINN: *(Indicating COREY)* Lucy.

LUCY: Corey? How are you?

COREY: They wouldn't assign me to a classroom.

LUCY: My God. Rest, Corey.

ERINN: You of all people.

COREY: There has to be a lesson in this.

(Offstage, a woman's voice begs, "No but I no but I no I have to have to have to....")

COREY: I'm fine. You're the ones.

(FARSTED enters.)

FARSTED: I spoke to the people in charge.

LUCY: Farsted, good for you. What's going to happen to the children?

FARSTED: These things have to be coordinated through a central authority. They're trying to learn the cause of it.

LUCY: I got here just as quick as I could. They called me up and said someone would need to identify them.

FARSTED: Now they're saying it could be a long time.

LUCY: I took everything off the refrigerator and stuffed it in a bag. Why did I do that?

ERINN: If you didn't put them in a bag they'd blow all over.

LUCY: Why bring them here? I must have had a reason.

FARSTED: The governor's man says they need the children for evidence about who did it.

LUCY: I can't believe someone meant this to happen.

ERINN: We have enemies. Not the town but I mean the state, or the country.

FARSTED: We stand for something.

ERINN: Some people are saying it's gangs.

FARSTED: Nah. Gangs? Not up here.

ERINN: Or a conspiracy.

LUCY: A conspiracy of who? Who's going to conspire against children?

FARSTED: They were our children. It could be against us.

LUCY: What have we done that anybody would conspire against us? We're not in charge of anything. What would be the point?

FARSTED: That's their thing—no point. So everybody's terrorized.

ERINN: They want everybody to be part of their war.

LUCY: This isn't a war. You know when you're in a war, you know it for a fact. Everyone has their duty to do. I was a girl, and by the end I was building munitions.

FARSTED: They won't let me do anything. Making me sit here and I've got jobs.

LUCY: In a war there are heroes all the time. You know their names.

ERINN: Farsted's father.

LUCY: More than our share. A lot of Gold Star mothers in this town. No. This was an accident. It has to be an accident.

FARSTED: Corey found them.

LUCY: Corey? Couldn't it have been an accident?

COREY: I don't know.

FARSTED: You didn't see who did it, did you?

COREY: No. Someone ought to know what I saw.

ERINN: Don't tell me.

LUCY: Me neither, for God's sake. I don't want to think of them like that.

ERINN: Think of how they've already arrived in paradise. Think of them in heaven.

(LUCY *takes artwork out of the bag.*)

LUCY: Corey, wasn't that funny last week when she brought me in to Show and Tell? Me telling the children about when irons were made of iron and we won the war? She'd bring home these paintings, I couldn't tell what they were supposed to be, she'd say, "Gran, it's *ob*viously a *cow*," or whatever it was.

ERINN: The minute they learn something they think they must have been the first ever to hear it, so they go try and teach it to you. "You know what, Mom? And you know what?"

(GAIL *breathes with increasing struggle.*)

LUCY: What is this, now? What did she tell me? I'll never know.

COREY: Lucy. Gail's going into shock.

LUCY: Gail? Honey? Rest easy now.

ERINN: She's in God's hands even this day, honey.

COREY: Farsted. Pick her up and carry her to the next room. There's a clinic.

(FARSTED *lifts* GAIL *in his arms.*)

LUCY: Careful, Farsted.

FARSTED: Gail? Come on with me, baby. You've gained a bit since high school, huh? I've got you. We're gone.

(FARSTED *exits, carrying* GAIL.)

ERINN: This world is so dangerous now. Everything's going along and suddenly it'll all—explode. Not for us to know.

(LUCY *begins gathering pictures into a pile.*)

LUCY: This wasn't the wisest thing to do.

ERINN: Now isn't that a pretty one.

LUCY: Isn't it? She painted a multicolored background and covered it all with black crayon, see? That's a whole crayon's worth. And then she scraped away lines in the black to expose the color behind it. That's how it comes out looking this way, with the multicolored lines. See? You're so clever with them, Corey. How do you get all these ideas for arts and crafts?

COREY: We try to pin down a scene or a feeling, a part of our memory. We pin it down, even if we bend it a little, even if there's no real life left in the thing at all. But maybe it reminds us of a living time, maybe it reminds us that we saw the scene, we felt the feeling, we were there. Maybe that bent-up thing on the piece of paper becomes one of the ways we recognize ourselves.

(*They are staring at her.*)

COREY: Arts and crafts. That's what we do in arts and crafts.

(COREY *exits.*)

ERINN: Is she going to be all right? With children?

LUCY: Yes.

ERINN: Fine. I was asking a question and I have been answered.

LUCY: And she's right. Lord above. I brought these because they said they were identifying the children, so I brought something to identify my granddaughter. My granddaughter is the one who did these. Grief makes you stupid. That's wrong, somehow. Do you feel stupid?

ERINN: Sure. Nothing new.

LUCY: Here's one she painted with just a line of plain white glue. You see? I think it's supposed to be herself. All in glue and then she shook the sparkles onto the paper. She showed me how she'd done it, all over the paper, and then turned the paper upside down, and shook it. I think that was her favorite part, shaking it. And turned it right side up again, and the drawing was all sparkles. She brought me the painting the day she made it. Sparkles in her hair, in her clothes. She said they'd been rained on her by the painting. Her mother had to wash all the clothes she wore that day by themselves, or those sparkles would have gotten into everything. She can act so spoiled, that child. Well. All spoiled, now. Well. Well. (*She brushes at her clothes*) All over me now. (*Pause*) I know what you're asking. She's a good teacher, but I wonder what they were learning from her.

(*The lights fade.*)

Scene Four

(SETH *pores over photographs and charts at the table.* COREY *enters, carrying her autoharp case, and watches him for a moment.*)

COREY: I bet I'm not supposed to be here. I couldn't sit there anymore, lot of grieving people.

SETH: I thought everyone here was waiting for remains to be released.

COREY: No.

SETH: You're not a parent?

COREY: I'm a teacher.

SETH: A teacher.

COREY: Yeah, that's me. Corey. I've got information.

SETH: Yes?

COREY: I need some help with this information.

SETH: Didn't anyone talk to you?

COREY: Somebody asked me some questions, but I don't think they were the right ones. Who are you?

SETH: My name is Seth. I'm in charge. Ann!

COREY: Good, because I've got to get this out of my head a little, I can't share my head with it, there isn't any room for me, and I'm going to have to leave.

SETH: Stay here. Talk to me.

COREY: Okay, until I get to the bottom of this, after that I don't know.

(ANN *enters.*)

ANN: Oh, Jesus, I'm sorry. Ma'am, if you come with me—

SETH: Ann, could I have a damp cloth, please? Warm.

(ANN *exits.*)

SETH: Do you have any idea who did it?

COREY: No.

SETH: Do you know what kind of device may have caused it?

COREY: No.

SETH: Well. The kinds of evidence we're interested in at this point come either from objects or from eyewitness accounts.

COREY: But I was right there.

SETH: Very close.

COREY: I saw the whole thing.

SETH: The aftermath.

COREY: I should have been killed.

SETH: But you weren't.

(ANN *enters with a damp cloth, which she hands to* SETH.)

SETH: Thank you.

(ANN *exits.* SETH *begins to swab the blood from* COREY's *forearms.*)

COREY: What are you doing?

SETH: You've got something on you. What are you carrying, there? That case.

COREY: Christ. This is an autoharp. Which I am carrying because the morning is supposed to start with music.

SETH: You've been carrying this around all day?

COREY: I left it in the teacher's lounge, and I told the children I'd go get it and be back in time for the bell. And I went there and got it and came back....

(SETH *holds the autoharp.*)

SETH: Corey. Your students are dead. They're all dead.

COREY: I saw.

(COREY *releases the autoharp, and* SETH *puts it on the table.*)

COREY: The door blew open, hit the wall, slammed back, shattered. I saw inside that doorframe for a fraction of a second and I remember thinking, "What's wrong with this picture?" It's a learning test, "What's wrong with this picture?" That's what we do, testing potential. I pulled the door free and went inside. Everything is wrong in this picture. Maybe you can help me, because they tell me school is closed, and if I can't learn something—my God, all my life—nursery school, elementary, secondary, high school, teachers college, student teacher, teacher—learning, up a grade, learning, up a grade, learning, if I can't do that...I need to learn why I'm not dead. Did the government send anyone here who can teach me why I'm not dead?

SETH: I'll try to find out.

COREY: The autoharp isn't much of an instrument. It's a handy instrument if you can't play an instrument, you just push the buttons for the chords. It keeps them in tune. (*She demonstrates pushing imaginary chord buttons on the lid of the case, singing:*)
In C major's fair city
Where D minor's so pretty
I C major my eyes on sweet Molly Malone...
(*Her voice trails off.*) I'd have thought I'd be crying by now.

SETH: You don't want to cry?

COREY: No.

SETH: Do you want to sleep?

COREY: No no no.

SETH: Are you hungry?

COREY: Wouldn't food make me sick?

SETH: Think about it.

COREY: I'm not hungry.

SETH: Do you want to be alone?

COREY: I want—can you believe this? I'm chatting about what I want.

SETH: What do you want?

COREY: I just *want*. I've got such a want.

(ANN *enters, carrying a plastic bag full of sharp metal shards.*)

ANN: Seth?

SETH: Yes, Ann.

ANN: Sharon wants to know if you recognize this.

SETH: Corey, shall I have Ann take you over now—

COREY: No. Don't make me go back and sit with those parents. I've been staring at their faces. Seeing their children's features. Ruined.

SETH: Stay here.

ANN: Seth?

SETH: Right. (*He studies the bag.*) Where'd she find this?

ANN: Sharon found it in the room, Iris found it in the bodies.

SETH: I've seen this stuff before. Where do I know this stuff?

ANN: You know this stuff?

SETH: This is one of ours. An old one. A couple of generations of weapon back. The shrapnel has a particular curl to the edges. It flies more wildly that way. It was someone's bright idea, it's the signature of this design. The characteristic ways it meets the body are documented in the literature. It did its job. I wonder who we gave it to.

COREY: Who could think of something like that?

SETH: Someone like me.

COREY: No. They must hate human life.

SETH: They can spot the flaws.

(SETH *writes on the bag as* SHARON *enters.*)

SHARON: (*To* ANN) There you are. Has the bomb squad finished searching?

ANN: Yes. They've done all the public buildings.

SETH: (*Holding the bag out to* SHARON) There's what you wanted to know.

SHARON: (*Taking the bag and handing him another, full of bits of brown stuff*) Great, I'll trade you. (*She reads his label.*) Yeah, I thought so. (*To* ANN) Did they turn up anything else?

ANN: No.

SETH: I want to know the minute someone claims responsibility. Thanks, Ann.

(ANN *exits.* SETH *examines the bag.*)

SETH: What is this?

SHARON: Bits of a mystery, thought you'd be interested. (*To* COREY) You're the teacher, right? Some kind of classroom thing? Science lesson?

COREY: I don't recognize it.

SETH: It's flesh.

SHARON: It's so old we weren't sure right away. At first we thought leather, but—

SETH: —leather doesn't have cartilage—

SHARON: Yeah. (*To* COREY:) Picture the room. Stuffed hamster? Mummified cat? Anything like that?

COREY: No. They've never given me money for science equipment. I spoke to the P T A.

SETH: I want this. All there is.

SHARON: There's lots of it, in little bits.

SETH: What distribution?

SHARON: Here.

(*She hands him a diagram. They bend over it.* COREY *tries to see, and can't. She wanders away, roaming the room.*)

SETH: It must have been very close to the epicenter.

SHARON: Look at the configuration.

(COREY *notices something on the wall.*)

SETH: Hm. What does it remind me of?

SHARON: I don't know.

COREY: Oh, my God. Oh, my God in heaven. I know what that is. That's a bone.

SETH: Clear through the wall.

SHARON: Ah, hell.

COREY: My God, my God, my God...

SETH: Ann!

SHARON: Terrible—

SETH: Senseless tragedy—

COREY: What would it *take*? To tear it off and then to... clear through the wall.

(ANN *enters.* COREY *has never taken her eyes off the bone.* SETH *has never taken his eyes off* COREY. SHARON *takes this in.*)

ANN: Seth? You called me?

SHARON: Tell Iris she forgot something, would you?

(ANN *exits.*)

SHARON: Seth. You want the rest of this stuff?

SETH: Yeah.

(SETH *puts the stuff back in the bag and hands it to* SHARON.)

SHARON: (*To* COREY:) You've got a sharp eye. Try not to call on God whenever you see something. He gets bored and stops listening. (*She exits.*)

COREY: The room blew up. I walked into it. Everyone came running. I stood in the doorway and I started barking orders. You—pull the fire alarm! You—get the kids out the doors! You—call the hospital, we need every ambulance in the county. And they went. Like a shot. Like I was an enormous shotgun. I felt—

SETH: Adrenaline.

COREY: I know adrenaline, I've been scared before. This—the whole place could have blown up and I could have taken it. I was...I was thrilled.

IRIS: (*Off*) Ann! See me in here, would you? (*She enters, carrying a pair of children's shoes in a plastic bag.*) No one seems to notice how their children are dressed. Last time they saw them alive and they can't picture them at all.

SETH: Corey. Would you excuse us, please?

(ANN *enters.*)

IRIS: These shoes don't match anyone's clothing list. Find out who they belong to.

ANN: How?

IRIS: Survivors are out there?

ANN: Yes.

IRIS: Show them the shoes.

SETH: It'll unhinge them.

ANN: There's blood on them.

IRIS: What do you want? We took the feet out.

SETH: Corey, it would be best if you left now.

COREY: No.

IRIS: If people give incomplete descriptions, they have to look at the actual effects. Serves 'em right.

SETH: The one who can identify them may be under sedation.

ANN: They're so little. Someone was proud to have tied these herself.

IRIS: Don't let your imagination get a mind of its own.

COREY: Those are Lydia's. She was proud of those shoes. She showed them off to everyone. Lydia Zuckerman.

IRIS: That's what we needed to know her by. Body 14. Good. One down.

SETH: You've got complete remains on this one?

IRIS: Enough to fill a coffin credibly. Closed coffin. (*To* COREY) Quick eye, there. Nice going.

(IRIS *and* ANN *exit.*)

SETH: You held together very well.

COREY: God, I must be detached. In my depths, you know? Down here. Down here I'm—

SETH: What's going on? Down there? Do you feel sick?

COREY: I must be sick, yeah, I must be one sick individual. It'll go away. (*Pause*) How recognizable are the children?

SETH: It varies wildly.

COREY: What if someone who knew them looked at them? To help the parents name them? So they wouldn't have to see so many. Would it spare them some pain?

SETH: You don't know what you're offering.

COREY: I've seen them. My memories of them are wrecked already.

SETH: If you're trying to help these children, spare yourself. Nothing we do and nothing we learn will ever save them. (*Pause*) I'll have to clear it with the others. Ann!

COREY: When people fight in wars, do they feel this way?

SETH: Some. The best ones.

COREY: What happens to them afterward?

(ANN *enters*.)

SETH: Would you get Iris and Sharon up here, please?

(ANN *exits*.)

SETH: I'll need you to wait outside while we talk this over.

COREY: Will you be there, too? Downstairs?

SETH: I'll be down there with you. I won't come up until you do.

COREY: I'll be in the hall. (*She turns to go.*)

SETH: Corey. Listen. I've had to learn what you're learning. There's a moment when you say, "All right. I decide on it. If I had it to do over, it would be what it is. This is what I actually wanted all along. Because I am not a victim things happen to. I am a person who learns. The more I can take in, the more complete I'll become. I will be a monster of knowledge. Let it all come."

(IRIS *and* SHARON *enter.*)

SETH: You might help us learn why they died.

COREY: Instead of me? I'd like to learn that. (*She exits.*)

SHARON: What are you up to?

SETH: I want her to look at the remains. The woman wants to help. And I think it'll help her.

SHARON: Help *her*? She is drunk with grief. Don't take advantage.

SETH: Think of all the false identifications it'll spare those pathetic people.

SHARON: Since when do you care about sparing anybody?

SETH: I'll take responsibility.

SHARON: I know you will.

SETH: She's tough.

SHARON: What are you, trying to build another of your own kind?

SETH: Iris? Should we let her see them?

IRIS: We've survived it. So can she.

SHARON: Oh, great. Solid advice from the Queen of the Dead.

(SETH *and* SHARON *laugh.*)

IRIS: Very funny.

(ANN *enters.*)

ANN: Excuse me—they can hear you out there.

SETH: Thanks, Ann. Sorry.

(SETH *and* ANN *exit.*)

SHARON: And he believed every word he said. He has no idea.

IRIS: God, that's frightening.

SHARON: Poor Seth.

IRIS: I liked her, too. She had a sharp eye.

SHARON: Poor thing.

IRIS: Well. Off we go.

(IRIS *and* SHARON *exit as the lights fade.*)

Scene Five

(FARSTED *is sitting at the table with his toolbox.* COREY *enters.*)

COREY: Farsted.

FARSTED: Corey.

COREY: What is that?

FARSTED: Belt sander. Don't see many this age still working.

COREY: What are you doing with it?

FARSTED: It's not working. Promised a man I'd have it for him. Fella refinishing thirty-five running feet of countertop, give me a couple days work. But this all happened and I'm supposed to be here, and I'm supposed to be there, so I thought I'd use the time. You don't think they'll care, do you?

COREY: No.

FARSTED: Some guys wouldn't bother, but you get known for conscientiousness, and there you are. Doing funny things.

COREY: What's the matter with it?

FARSTED: Belonged to my father, I think the bearings are fouled, he always took care of his tools, but you get a name for conscientiousness, you work in all weathers.

COREY: Let me see it. (*She takes the sander.*) Was your father conscientious, too?

FARSTED: He was a war hero. Before I was born. In combat you're conscientious or you're dead. He kicked back after that. Those bearings are in sad shape.

COREY: Yeah, the tracking's off. Give me a hunk of that steel wool, would you?

FARSTED: (*Passing a piece of steel wool*) Here you go. So what about my boy?

COREY: They're working on it. Lot of smart people in there. From the city? Quick.

FARSTED: What about you?

COREY: What about me?

FARSTED: I thought you'd be working on it. They were your class, right?

COREY: Right. Yeah, I'll be helping.

FARSTED: Nice for you.

COREY: How you figure?

FARSTED: Guys from the city. Successful.

COREY: You got some oil in there?

FARSTED: I'll shoot some. They know how they did it yet? The terrorists or whoever?

COREY: You think it was terrorists?

FARSTED: It's happening all over. Thought we'd be safe up here, raise the kids. Some guys would of left, go down and work for the aerospace. Lot of guys gone. Me, I thought—

COREY: Conscientious.

FARSTED: Keep the family out of the way, take care of my old man.

COREY: He died, didn't he?

FARSTED: Liver thing, took years. He was tough. Combat Marine.

COREY: There's a plug under here.

FARSTED: Got it. Try it out.

(COREY *guns the sander. She stares at the flying surface of the sandpaper as it runs down.*)

COREY: I've been having them do a unit on their grandparents for Show and Tell.

(COREY *hands the sander back to* FARSTED.)

FARSTED: Did my boy do good in school?

COREY: He was very conscientious.

(*Pause*)

FARSTED: I'd better go back to that man's kitchen.

(FARSTED *exits.* COREY *stands and crosses downstage, singing under her breath.*)

COREY: She died of a fever
And no one could save her
And that was the end of sweet Molly Malone....

(*The faint hissing and knocking are heard, and repeat now and then.*)

COREY: Today we'll start our historical dioramas. To make a diorama you start with a shoe box and you think of a picture of history. I'll give you an example of a diorama. (*As she thinks for a moment, the light grows colder.*) There's a streetcorner in the town where I went to school. Across the street from a little park with a couple of trees. A little lawn. I remember a time I was standing there. I'd always gotten a weird feeling at that corner—not always every time, but often. It was five-thirty and it was the middle of the winter. I was about to meet someone. (*She smiles.*) Yes, a boy. (*The smile fades.*) I was standing and staring at a tree across the way. Thinking how black the tree was, full of black leaves. And then there was a sound, and the tree shook and a whole flock of birds rose out of it, hundreds of birds all of a sudden, this black shape up in the sky, and left the tree behind.

(*During the following, the three women enter, wearing large white lab coats, their hands in their pockets.*)

COREY: And I felt like when I left that corner, and went where I was supposed to go next—you know what it was? That I was looking at this world for the last time, because when I left that corner and went where I was about to go, that the world would be, I don't know, a different color from now on. So I stood there. Yeah, pretty spooky. So I might take a shoe box and put in a little person and a curb and a tree suddenly stripped of a skyful of birds, and that's the way I'd make my diorama.

(SETH *enters and crosses down to her. They look at each other as the lights crossfade to:*)

Scene Six

(*One stark beam of light as from down a long hall.* SETH *and* COREY *stand in the doorway. The three women are dimly visible.*)

SETH: Can you see what's in this room?

COREY: No.

SETH: Good. This is going to be a long bad day, and then it'll be over. Listen to me closely. There is a way of looking that I've learned. You can stare directly at them

and barely see them at all. I'll tell you how to do it and
when you're ready you'll turn on the lights.

COREY: I'll never get over this.

SETH: No. You'll get through it. Are you listening?

COREY: Go ahead.

SETH: In the explosion, it's as if their names, their
identities have been thrown free of their bodies. So
we look at the teeth, the fillings. We look at the bones,
for old fractures. We get sex from the pelvis if intact.
Race from the cheekbones and jaw and brow. The
identification blows away. The fingerprints are the first
to go. Hands and feet are so ephemeral. We're grateful
for a face. This room contains information. Not people
anymore. Remember that and you'll be fine.

COREY: Where's the light?

SETH: The switch is behind you. Feel?

COREY: Yes.

SETH: Whenever you're ready. To start with,
concentrate on not seeing anything. Then see only
what is here.

COREY: Their troubles are done.

SETH: Nothing but evidence.

COREY: Their troubles are done.

SETH: Nothing but information. There are no people
here.

(A switch clicks. Moonlight on the three women.)

IRIS: Oh, my back.

SHARON: Big Dipper.

ANN: Where?

SHARON: See?

IRIS: Ursa Major.

SHARON: What?

ANN: Big Bear.

SHARON: How did they get a bear out of that?

IRIS: I wonder if they've moved since then?

ANN: The people?

IRIS: Which people?

ANN: Naming-things people.

IRIS: I wonder if the stars have moved.

SHARON: People haven't moved, we're where we've always been.

ANN: What are some other ones?

IRIS: Let's see....

ANN: The North Star, you go two up from which ones?

IRIS: I can't remember.

ANN: Those, I think. See?

IRIS: There's one like a "W" somewhere, where is that? Five stars together.

SHARON: Which are together and which are apart?

IRIS: Cassiopeia. There's a story about it.

SHARON: They all look together to me.

ANN: The night is so clear. There are so many.

SHARON: I don't see a "W".

ANN: What's the story?

IRIS: She's a queen in a chair and she can't get out of it. Her daughter's another constellation—do you remember the name? Something bad happens to her.

SHARON: The queen?

IRIS: Her daughter. But the queen has to watch.

ANN: In the sky.

SHARON: How do they get a queen in a chair out of five stars like a "W"?

ANN: How do you get a "W"?

SHARON: You find what you look for.

IRIS: Whoever named the stars was very morbid.

SHARON: They're millions of miles apart. They don't have anything to do with each other.

IRIS: They had powerful imaginations.

SHARON: I don't see a "W" at all.

IRIS: It's probably below the horizon this time of year.

ANN: They're beautiful.

IRIS: The light is very old, you know. It's energy from a long time ago. They could all be gone by now.

ANN: I don't understand how the light can be so bright when it's had to come so far.

SHARON: I think I'm getting cold.

IRIS: There's Orion.

SHARON: Where?

ANN: The Hunter.

IRIS: He's a belt and a sword.

ANN: I see him.

SHARON: Where?

IRIS: Follow my arm.

SHARON: There? Those?

IRIS: There.

SHARON: I see him! How about that.

(The lights fade on the three women.)

Scene Seven

(The moon is down. As the scene goes on, it gets steadily darker, until SETH *and* COREY *are visible only in silhouette.)*

SETH: Go home. Go to sleep.

COREY: I'm not tired, I wish I were tired, I'm not.

SETH: How do you feel?

COREY: Great, I should be struck dead for how I feel.

SETH: You've made all the difference. You're extraordinarily observant.

COREY: What kind of person—

SETH: You put yourself through hell—

COREY: I couldn't stop looking! Don't *thank* me. Christ. It was...fascinating.

SETH: You wanted to help. You hoped it would justify your survival. You did help. Others will suffer less. What are you ashamed of?

COREY: I thought I'd get rid of this—I thought by now—

SETH: What? Get rid of what? *(Pause)* All right. This may seem like a strange question, it may not: In a crisis like this, some people discover a physical desire. Not toward any object. Just a need. It would be completely normal. You almost lost your life. Your life is asserting itself. Or perhaps your case is different.

(Pause)

COREY: The longer this day goes on, the more I horrify myself.

SETH: Completely normal. Look. People have some surprising things inside them. And I don't mean the contents of their skins. You saw Iris and her staff taking all those photographs of the remains?

COREY: Thousands of them.

SETH: All those shutters clicking, sounded like a plague of locusts down there, didn't it? Several people on the staff collect those photographs.

COREY: As evidence.

SETH: They bootleg prints.

COREY: They collect them?

SETH: They keep scrapbooks. It's no good trying to stop them. They trade with their friends around the country, some of them. It's a hobby. Photos of notorious carnage.

COREY: Why? Why collect photographs of mutilated bodies?

SETH: They find it...fascinating.

COREY: I've got to ask you a question. You see these things all the time, you live with them in your head, you have friends and...a wife or whatever. You sleep and eat.

SETH: What's your question?

COREY: How?

SETH: How can I do this?

COREY: It's none of my business.

SETH: No, it's just...somebody has to, and I have a knack for it.

COREY: I'm keeping you from your work.

SETH: Do you want to go home?

COREY: I don't want to look at anything familiar right now.

SETH: We have beds set up here. Take one.

COREY: I'd better not. Seth, I've got to do something.

SETH: You've done something. You've survived.

COREY: I've got to do something else.

SETH: Is there someone you can call? A husband or whatever?

COREY: No, no husband or whatever. Not in this town. Men here...men here leave here. They go south and look for work building aircraft, or they stay in the mill and fester.

SETH: You're not from here?

COREY: Another little town, you wouldn't know its name.

SETH: I probably would.

COREY: My condolences. There was a job here, not many jobs in the world right now. What about you, are you married?

SETH: A long time ago, not anymore. There aren't many people where I work either.

COREY: You live in the city?

SETH: Once in a while.

COREY: How do people survive the speed of it? It must be exciting.

SETH: It can be...fascinating.

COREY: And you can go to the museum whenever you want.

SETH: Yes.

COREY: I would think that that would help. In my room, I have some postcards from the museum. I mounted them in old picture frames and hung them on the walls. They help me, sometimes.

SETH: Which artists? In your room?

COREY: Oh, Dürer, Vermeer. I think Dürer is just the right name for Dürer, don't you? Durable, endurance. Those firm lines.

SETH: Yes.

COREY: Vermeer is my great love. Those women working under open windows. I keep him in the kitchen, to remind me of the beautiful in the everyday.

SETH: Have you lived in the city?

COREY: I've always been drawn to it. I knew an artist from the city once. A boy. He painted me.

SETH: Did he.

COREY: One night we got very drunk on Burgundy wine, and he painted me. He started watercoloring my nails and kept on going and pretty soon I was festooned with watercolor. He was so gentle, camelhair brushes, so smooth. The only night of my life I've had camelhair on my skin. I thought I knew what a masterpiece would feel, so attended to, every millimeter of my surface attended to and thought out and eyed and touched. The colors didn't fade completely for weeks. I think I had to shed that entire set of skin before it went away. The—feeling you asked me about before.

SETH: Perfectly normal.

COREY: It might be back. I just wanted to warn you.

SETH: It's got nothing to do with me. You should try to sleep.

COREY: How can you live with this?

SETH: How do I live with myself? (*Pause*) I hope I'll do some good. I started in government because it seemed so graceful, when I was young, imposing harmony. Now I just try to contain the chaos. I'm supposed to learn the cause of this disaster. To keep it from happening again. But it won't happen again. These children won't die anymore. So all I can do.... Everyone, sooner or later, stands at a doorway and cries, "Someone I love is in there, let me in." And somebody has to say, no, you can't go in there. We strike a bargain. I'll never see her alive again. Can I settle for her dead? I'll give her a burial place. I'll give her a place in my memory. Is it a deal? Can I live with this? Stay sane? Keep working? Can I walk away? People like me—like us—our job is to stand in some doorway the dead have gone through, and turn the living back. No one will remember we were there. My days are full. But how I live with *myself*.... I guess what I hope is that I don't. You should go to sleep.

COREY: So should you.

SETH: It really would be wiser if we went to bed.

COREY: Each of us? Both of us? *(Pause)* I don't do this. It isn't me at all.

SETH: It isn't me either.

COREY: Your skin, it's like a child's. Here inside your wrist. So gentle. It's like it's never gone through anything.

SETH: Look, though. The veins and the bones come right through.

COREY: This baby skin wrapped around this old arm. Please would you open my blouse?

SETH: Would you like to move somewhere more comfortable?

COREY: No. The catch is in the front.

SETH: There we are. Beautiful.

COREY: I have inverted nipples. My breasts were my disappointment with my body, I'm afraid.

SETH: Not to me.

COREY: Now the—oh!

SETH: What?

COREY: Never mind, you found it for yourself.

SETH: Is that all right?

COREY: Yes. That's good. Something you should know. I've been told that I weep. If it happens, don't be scared, okay?

SETH: Okay.

COREY: Look into my eyes?

(Whatever light is left fades.)

END OF ACT ONE

ACT TWO

Scene One

(IRIS *and* ANN *are sitting at the table.)*

IRIS: Really?

ANN: Really. Please, I'm fascinated.

IRIS: Well. What I do is get to know all the people.

ANN: Do you divide them up among your team?

IRIS: You can't. That's the point. It has to be one mental picture. One mind, holding it all.

ANN: Like blindfold chess?

IRIS: Precisely. Precisely!

(SHARON *enters.)*

SHARON: Yes I'm late, sorry, let's get started. Where is he?

IRIS: We're waiting for him.

SHARON: Hey, I stop for his goddamn staff meetings, he can, too.

IRIS: He, uh—they haven't come down yet this morning.

SHARON: He and the—oy oy oy.

ANN: I guess this isn't like him? They talk about how driven he is.

IRIS: No, this is not like him.

SHARON: No. This *is* him. I've got facts to consolidate and he's off playing Hide the Body Part. (*She watches* ANN.*)* She blushes. I love it.

IRIS: We were talking. Yes, it is like playing blindfold chess.

SHARON: Iris. Really?

ANN: Iris was telling me about mental pictures.

IRIS: Sculpture.

SHARON: I bet.

IRIS: The model for the identification of a group of bodies would resemble a three-dimensional transparent solid—

ANN: A glass cube?

IRIS: Yes. Gridded in all dimensions. One axis—across the top—would be the names of all the victims, Allen through Zuckerman. A second axis—say down the side—would be the numbers assigned to all the bodies, one through twenty-four. The third axis—the depth—it would be easiest to imagine as many sheets of glass, every sheet representing a trait.

SHARON: You figure that woman's a coroner groupie?

IRIS: Sharon, people are trying to hold a mental image here.

SHARON: Yeah, me, too. I don't see her as a coroner groupie though.

IRIS: This girl wants to learn something. Take a trait. Say, orthodontia.

ANN: Braces?

IRIS: Right. You talk to the families and find out which names wore braces. You look at the bodies, you see which are wearing braces. Each sheet of glass is a grid of squares. Each square represents the coordinate of a name and a body. If a square represents the conjunction of a braces name and a body with no braces, that's no good, and you black it out. If a square represents the conjunction of a body with braces and a name without, that's no good either, and you black *that* out. But if a square represents a name with braces and a body with braces, you leave the glass clear. Likewise if a square has an unbraced name and an unbraced body. You leave your square of glass transparent. You have a question?

ANN: What's a coroner groupie?

IRIS: A very rare pathological aberration.

SHARON: Death camp followers. The pillow talk defies description.

IRIS: Shut up, Sharon.

SHARON: One of them wanted to lie absolutely still while I—

IRIS: Shut up, Sharon.

ANN: You use a different plate of glass for each trait?

IRIS: Precisely. Thank you. Sex, if it can be determined—shut *up*, Sharon—eye color likewise; hair color, which you can look at subcutaneously even if the hairs themselves have burnt away. If there's a match between body and name, leave a clear space. Then when you have a deep enough axis of traits, you look at your solid and see where the light shines through. And there's your identity. Got it? Not that it's ever that simple in real life.

ANN: How can you get to know a roomful of dead people?

IRIS: Don't get superior.

ANN: I wasn't.

IRIS: They're dead and you're alive, and aren't you the uppity one.

ANN: Really, I didn't—

IRIS: Fear. That's all. Fear. Our goal is to be objective.

SHARON: Yeah. So much easier than being people.

IRIS: Don't knock objects. Objects were here before we were and they'll be here long after we're gone. In the meantime we exploit them. We make them more and more dangerous. Most of our work is viewing the result of a person losing an encounter with an object. And we always lose in the end.

(SETH *enters. They all look at him.*)

SETH: So. Morning.

SHARON: Thank you.

SETH: Staff meeting, five minutes.

SHARON: Yes, sir.

SETH: Shut up, Sharon. (*He exits.*)

ANN: May I ask you both a favor?

SHARON: Sure.

ANN: Would the two of you recommend that I be assigned to this section permanently? I did my internship with the Maintenance Department? This is a lot more interesting than the Maintenance Department, you know? This beats the hell out of the Maintenance Department.

(*The women remain as the lights change.*)

Scene Two

(IRIS, SHARON, *and* ANN *become* LUCY, ERINN, *and* GAIL.
GAIL's *head is on her hand, which covers one of her eyes.*
FARSTED *enters, carrying a paper bag and drinking a beer.*
He crumples his beer can in his hands. He reaches into the
bag, takes another beer and opens it.)

LUCY: She's not a bad woman, really. Not spiteful.

ERINN: No?

LUCY: Just loose with herself.

ERINN: I didn't say cast her out. Live and let live.
But that she can live, and others be taken away from
us, that frets me terribly. Why was she spared? All
those innocent children dead, and she of all people
preserved.

LUCY: It's a miracle anyone survived.

ERINN: It's a senseless miracle. I've said it.

LUCY: She's very creative.

ERINN: Is that creativity? Dancing on the graves of
children? People can be creative and still know right
from wrong.

(COREY *enters. A long moment in which* COREY *feels no one*
speaking to her or acknowledging her presence.)

FARSTED: How are you doing?

COREY: Bearing up.

FARSTED: Good. That's good.

COREY: And you?

FARSTED: I'm grieving. You know.

COREY: Gail. How are you?

(GAIL *lifts her head. She has a black eye.*)

COREY: Gail, what happened? Are you okay?

GAIL: Isn't it stupid? It's funny, when it happened I had a second there saying, "Oh great, my daughter's dead and now I'm going to have a black eye." It's the medication. Makes me goof up. Really really really stupid mistake with a cabinet door. Ben put in these cabinets?

COREY: How is Ben?

GAIL: They ought to give Ben some medication. Ha ha ha ha ha. See what he does then. He, boy, he just stood there, going, "Where's my little girl?" saying, "You had her last, where is she?" (*Touching the eye*) Cabinet door, boom. Stupid.

(*Pause*)

COREY: Lord above. Lucy?

(LUCY *turns to face her.*)

COREY: Are you still speaking to me?

LUCY: Could I see her?

COREY: Lucy, if you knew—an event like this—the condition of the remains—

LUCY: Was she blown to pieces? Just say so.

COREY: Yes.

(*Pause*)

LUCY: Back in the war they warned us in the factory what would happen if someone messed up. Put the fear of God in us girls. Seems wrong for it to happen to a little child.

COREY: Yeah.

ERINN: Corey? Can I ask you something?

COREY: Go ahead.

ERINN: You're not a God-fearing woman at all.

COREY: No.

ERINN: Think of that. Think of that. And He's killed my child.

COREY: And let me live.

ERINN: Yeah. Yeah, He did.

LUCY: Erinn. Honey.

COREY: And you think I'm happy about that.

ERINN: I've always tried to see His hand beneath my blessings. Blame the trials on Satan. I don't see what I could have done to bring this punishment down on that little boy. I doted on that boy.

COREY: They say He's jealous. He said so Himself.

(ERINN *slaps* COREY *across the face.*)

COREY: You're right. What a clever thing to say.

ERINN: Is that what it means. All my love, only for Him, leave your family, follow only Me. Well. That is petty. I'm sorry, but that is very small. If I have to love nothing in the world, or He'll take it from me, the way He has, again and again, He does this and says, "Turn to Me for comfort." Sick, in a way. I mean—is that what it meant, all along? Is that what He needs? That's pathetic. Men are His image, that's all I can say.

COREY: Have you thought He wanted your son with Him in heaven?

ERINN: You don't believe that.

COREY: No.

LUCY: I do, Erinn, I'm sure it's true.

ERINN: He didn't need that boy. He has angels galore. Spite. Spite. But I tell you: That boy had better be in heaven, because if he isn't, I'll go looking for him. I'll find him, too. I'll have all eternity to search in. I'll call his name from one end of it to the other, from the blackest pit up to God's own face, and if that boy doesn't have his just place, I'll see to it. I will set things right in heaven. Because I tell you: It's high time—high time—someone taught God about justice. (*She exits.*)

LUCY: She didn't mean it.

COREY: Sure she did. I can't find any sense to it either. Me being here.

LUCY: Here in town?

COREY: I've been trying. Once we find out what happened, and I can get back in a classroom—

LUCY: Back in a classroom.

COREY: Well, I mean—that's what I do.

LUCY: Don't you think there might be questions about that?

COREY: What do you mean?

LUCY: Corey, I've always told everyone what a wonderful teacher you are, but.... Do you think there are any classrooms free? The town doesn't have much money as it is, we can't just put you in an empty classroom, which is what we'd have to do, because, I mean, there's one less group of students in the school now, and it was yours.

COREY: Do you think—do you really think they would—

LUCY: Maybe it would be easier somewhere else?

COREY: I'm the teacher whose class blew up. It's going to make for an ambiguous letter of recommendation.

LUCY: There must be something else you can do?

COREY: I've got no system but the school system.

LUCY: There might be a way, after this blows over—

COREY: No. You're saying that now, but a second ago you said the opposite. They'll never let me back—

LUCY: Corey, I'd better check on Erinn, she—

COREY: —this is the last classroom I'll ever see, this one here, when I walk out of here, I won't know where to put myself, because the thing is—the thing—the thing is that I teach.

LUCY: Corey, I have to go.

COREY: What do you want me to do?

LUCY: I'm sure you'll think of the right thing. (*She exits.*)

COREY: What do you want me to do?!

(*Pause*)

FARSTED: You want a beer?

COREY: What?

FARSTED: We could go outside if you wanted to.

COREY: Now? I'm—

FARSTED: Sit, drink a beer. Right outside. You'd hear him call.

COREY: Where's your wife?

FARSTED: She's down the hall with people watching her. They've given her something so she doesn't scream anymore. She chuckles a lot. Does it by the hour. Where's your government man? (*Pause*) Nobody's holding anything against each other, huh? Would I be talking to you? Offering you a beer?

COREY: Why are you?

FARSTED: I thought—a time like this, people know each other better. You got troubles, I got troubles. You knew my boy, we could talk about my boy. What I'm asking—how do you talk to that guy? What did you say so he knew what you wanted?

COREY: I don't want to drink on the ground. Sitting on the dirt and drinking, that's too sad.

FARSTED: We're supposed to be sad. Come on, if he said, "Let's take a seat here on the lawn and drink champagne," you'd go. I can see why you'd do that.

COREY: Can you?

FARSTED: I'm trying to. I mean—what have you got there? Is he your ride out of here or what?

COREY: He's learning things. Some people do that.

FARSTED: I need to learn something. Can you teach me something?

COREY: I should leave.

FARSTED: We could both leave. You want to leave? I'll walk you.

COREY: You're scaring me, Farsted. All right?

FARSTED: I'm not trying to scare you, I need to ask you something!

COREY: Why are you threatening me?

FARSTED: I'm sitting here. I haven't raised a hand. I'd never.

COREY: I don't know that.

FARSTED: You got powerful friends. Squash me like a snail on the sidewalk, that guy.

COREY: He's here to learn what happened is all.

FARSTED: Yeah. Yeah. So you talk to him. You two are probably so good at talking that's all it takes. You get good enough at doing a thing. Guys I know—you know too, I won't name who, don't want to tempt you—guys fix up a car so good, they do it *that* way. Muscle car, put a woman on the passenger side, go fast enough, get those low vibrations. They tell me,

I wouldn't know—they have to hose down the seats after? Talking, this guy, same way I bet.

COREY: You're hurting me, Farsted, why?

FARSTED: I'm asking a question. You and him, you— talk. Information rubs off. So maybe you know how things like—with these dead bodies. What's the rule?

COREY: What rule?

FARSTED: I don't know, I'm asking you. If somebody's got dead bodies, how long are they allowed to keep them?

COREY: How long are they allowed—

FARSTED: Or anybody. Anybody with dead parts. Do they get in trouble?

COREY: Will he get in trouble?

FARSTED: Or anybody.

COREY: I don't understand what you're asking.

FARSTED: I'm trying to learn something and I don't know what it is.

COREY: If somebody holds onto dead bodies—

FARSTED: Or parts even.

COREY: Will somebody get in trouble if they hold onto dead body parts for a long time?

FARSTED: You did it. That's the thing I don't know.

COREY: I don't know either. How long are we talking about?

FARSTED: Say years. Years and years for instance.

COREY: I don't think it'll take him anything like that long.

FARSTED: You never know.

COREY: I could ask. I could try to learn for you.

FARSTED: No, no, don't try to learn for me. I was hoping you'd know. (*He exits.*)

GAIL: I'm sorry. I fell asleep. Did they all go? I'm sorry. I saw you. Last night. When I opened the door. I saw you sleeping.

COREY: Sleeping.

GAIL: It looked like you were. He was sleeping. I didn't mean to. I just opened the wrong door, I'd been over getting another pill, and I was walking back, and these pills keep making me do stupid things with doors.

COREY: And you saw me.

GAIL: Both of you. Afterward, I guess. Asleep, all—together.

COREY: Gail. You told them, didn't you?

GAIL: I never tell. Oh, the—what I saw.

COREY: Why?

GAIL: I guess—I must have had to.

COREY: Yeah.

GAIL: I'm sorry.

COREY: It happens. Why don't you go back to sleep now.

GAIL: Thanks. I hope so.

COREY: Were you dreaming?

GAIL: No. It was nice. Just—no.

(COREY *exits.* GAIL *lowers her head. The lights fade.*)

Scene Three

(SETH *is working at the table.* COREY *enters.*)

COREY: I need to ask you something.

SETH: Hi.

(COREY *and* SETH *embrace.*)

COREY: Listen. People know.

SETH: And they're unhappy about it.

COREY: Oh boy.

SETH: And this matters to you.

COREY: They think I don't care what happened to their children. It was bad enough I'm still alive, but now.... I know these people. I should have known how they expect you to behave in a disaster. I did know.

SETH: You tried. You couldn't act that way.

COREY: I'll never get them to understand this, I can't tell them the truth, they'll never want to hear it, they'd rather I just—they'd rather not have to look at me. Everyone I meet—they look at me—and I don't make any sense. I'm sorry. This is not even slightly fascinating. It's just—Farsted was out there ranting at me about parts of the body. Saying somebody might get in trouble. It was crazed, it was very deeply crazed. I guess he's been unhappy in his family a long time. But he's never.... (*Pause*) I think I know something.

SETH: Tell me.

COREY: I don't know if I should. I don't want to be wrong about this.

SETH: Tell me.

COREY: I wanted them to love history, so they would learn it. I thought, who do children love better than their grandparents?

SETH: Their grandparents are history in person....

COREY: Their grandparents have saved things from the past.

SETH: Souvenirs.

COREY: I said, if you're very careful, and get permission, this is what we'll do in Show and Tell.

SETH: Whose turn was it that day to bring things in?

COREY: Tommy Farsted.

SETH: Whose grandfather was—

COREY: A war hero.

SETH: A souvenir is an object charged with time. If matter is energy in a different state, is time energy, too? Burning so slowly. We didn't identify any of the bodies as Tommy Farsted. He isn't here.

COREY: He ran away. He brought something in and ran away.

SETH: This still doesn't make enough sense, it still doesn't account for all of the damage. Christ. I'm going to have to put it all back together, aren't I? All right then. (*He refers to photographs and charts on the table. He moves around the room, acting out with an arm or a leg the moves he describes.*) Would it be possible that—if her arm ends up there—

(*As* SETH *mentally replaces the bodies where they fell,* COREY *watches them die.*)

COREY: Lydia—

SETH: —and the torso—

COREY: Christopher—

SETH: —here. Turned this way? Explosion! I'm spun so, hit that tow-headed—

COREY: Kenny—

SETH: —desk fragment—is there? —*that* one, the legs to the knee—

COREY: Greta—

SETH: —flies *across*, takes the arm and spine—

COREY: Cyndi—

SETH: —so, the torso underneath—

COREY: Robby—

SETH: —here. But explain the disembowelment of this one.

COREY: Katey—

SETH: I explain it thus: *(He begins his dance of death, flying around the room, the impacts more and more violent.)* I'm here. Facing front, no, back to the *that's* right. Piece of the desk, edge on, lumbar-to-hips flies like—

COREY: Phillip—

SETH: —rips in this direction, flight path, *so*, legs across the—

COREY: Nancy—

SETH: —Yes of course, and thus the crumpled heap—

COREY: Steve—

SETH: Now. What did this? Could it be—whose is this? Who does this belong to? No, no, clearly, look—she's embedded in that one—

COREY: Paul—

SETH: —facing that way, why is this one facing away?

COREY: Cath—

SETH: Sees what's coming? Scared? Anthropomorphic garbage, the *pieces*, eyes on the *pieces*. Look, here, see what you know. The girl with the cast on her arm.

COREY: Lynn—

SETH: Taken, into the wall, hence the—head—

COREY: Dan—

SETH: —foot—

COREY: Ben—

SETH: —pelvic—

COREY: Curt—

SETH: —*yes*, so *what* made the, this, and here, and all the— shrapnel, no, debris, no, another body, maybe, but where *is* it? All right. Where would it have had to be?

(SETH *moves with a new urgency.* COREY *begins to walk slowly toward a particular spot.*)

COREY: Tommy?

SETH: Let's say here, standing behind the—explosion! No, there'd be some of me here. Standing on top of— explosion! No, the ceiling, did they check—nothing in the ceiling here so—

COREY: Tommy?

(SETH *has arrived very close behind* COREY.)

SETH: Here. Right smack *here*, I'm—what if I'm—

COREY: Holding the mine.

SETH: (*Grasping her in his arms*) Yes!

COREY: *Finish it.*

SETH: I'm cradling it, I'm that close, with it, showing it, I've brought this to show you, oh my God he blew up in their faces! I'm Farsted, it's my turn, I've put them in a wagon, dragged them in, picked up this land mine. Look. See. A few get scared, a few move toward me. Maybe I slip—maybe I pull something—maybe I've never been very happy in school. So Farsted is here,

and I'm Farsted—explosion! I'm blown to bits. Yes!
Done it!

(COREY *sobs in terrible pain as* SETH *holds her.*)

COREY: All gone all gone all gone all gone all gone...

SETH: Ann!

(ANN *enters.*)

SETH: Have Mister Farsted brought in. Tell Iris and
Sharon to come up. And tell them to bring that old
flesh they found.

(ANN *exits.*)

COREY: Not one of them absent. Not one. All gone.
When I teach...when I taught. On the good days, we
all—oh, the energy flies, your body tingles, you could
almost smell the ozone. The children store that energy,
they can run on it for years. All gone. It never occurred
to me—I put something in his mind. It started ticking.
That was the cause of this whole thing. My cause.

SETH: Stop now.

COREY: My great cause.

SETH: Stop. Tommy Farsted had four grandparents.
What caused him to want to tell about this one? What
caused the explosion in your classroom instead of
somewhere else along the way? It could have been the
street, it could have been the hallway. Corey, don't
take this on. Believe me. Please believe me. There's no
reason to it.

(COREY *removes herself from his arms.*)

COREY: I should go home. Those people need you to be
done.

SETH: Where are you going?

COREY: I said I'd stay here long enough to learn what
happened. Now I've learned. I know my mistakes.

That Show and Tell assignment, that was one mistake.
And leaving the room. I'll never make that mistake
again. So now I know. Thank you.

(ANN *enters.*)

SETH: For what?

COREY: For answering my question.

SETH: Which question was that?

COREY: The reason I'm not dead. You're right. There's
no reason at all.

SETH: When I'm finished here, I'll come find you. All
right? Corey? All right?

(*She's gone.*)

ANN: Seth. They're ready for you.

SETH: Right, thanks...

(*ANN exits. SETH gathers his papers.*)

SETH: Good work...

(*As SETH exits, the lights fade.*)

Scene Four

(COREY *is pacing, feeling the air with a still hand. The
hissing sound is much louder. Behind the table the three
women are sitting, dimly visible. Light shows around the
door, and grows brighter through the rest of the scene. Three
loud knocks.*)

COREY: Science. Remember the experiment we did with
the candle in the bottle? Where as long as the flame
was alive it kept poisoning and poisoning the air in
the bottle until the flame put itself out? Remember
how we had to make sure there weren't any leaks, or it
wouldn't work? This is like that. A room is a container,

like a bottle, or a box. Doors sealed, windows sealed.
Think of your body as a bottle with your self inside.

(*Three loud knocks, and "Corey" called faintly*)

COREY: And once you've done all that, you can wait,
and look at your Vermeer. If you stare a long time,
the people in the painting seem to breathe. Long after
we've stopped, they'll still be seeming that way.

(*Three loud knocks*)

COREY: He's painted an open window, and you think, I
should close that window, or this won't work. But you
can't. That window's going to be open forever. (*She
shakes her head and sinks to her knees.*) So it's good. You
sit in front of your painting, and feel the breeze in your
face. It's all right.

(*Pounding now, three times, and "Corey!" called more
loudly*)

COREY: Wait a minute. The breeze in your—no. Fresh
air, that isn't right. You don't want fresh air. You want
to leave the gas on. Huh. There's a trick to killing
yourself. You have to learn everything backwards.
I've never heard that. That's interesting. I bet there's a
lesson in that. (*She tries to stand and sinks back.*) I should
teach that to people. They'll be interested. Oh, right. I'll
be dead.

(*Pounding, three times. "Corey!"*)

COREY: Wait. Somebody's out there. (*She looks toward
the source of the pounding.*) If I open the door, I could tell
them.

(*Pounding, five times, as the lights fade*)

Scene Five

(SETH, SHARON, *and* IRIS *are around* FARSTED *at the table.*)

SETH: Please, Mr Farsted.

FARSTED: I don't know.

SETH: Mr Farsted, we have the truth already, all we want from you is confirmation. I'll ask you again: Do you want a lawyer?

FARSTED: No lawyer.

SETH: He'd be someone on your side.

FARSTED: Who picks him?

SETH: The government.

FARSTED: Who pays him?

SETH: The government. But he'd be on your side.

FARSTED: No. Thank you.

SETH: Mr Farsted, your friends and neighbors—the parents of your son's classmates—they are desperate for answers. Please don't make them wait any longer.

FARSTED: I just don't know.

SETH: All right, then. Sharon?

(SHARON *holds up the bag of brown stuff.*)

SHARON: I want to show you something, Mr Farsted. Have you ever seen these before?

FARSTED: I don't know.

SHARON: Do you know what they are?

FARSTED: I can't tell.

SHARON: We found these bits of old flesh. We were able to reconstruct a couple of them. (*She shows him a smaller bag.*) Look. Can you tell what that is?

FARSTED: I'm not sure.

SHARON: Name it! I want to see your stupid mouth make its name!

FARSTED: Ear.

SHARON: What?

FARSTED: It's an ear.

SHARON: Is it? It's got a hole in it. See? This one does, too. Not here... (*Her finger approaches his ear.*) ...where the sound goes into the head. Not here... (*Her finger nearly touches his earlobe.*) ...where you might have it pierced for decoration. But here.

(SHARON *touches the upper part of* FARSTED's *ear. He jerks his head away.*)

SHARON: They're all like that. And this piece here, what is this?

FARSTED: Wire. Through the hole.

IRIS: They're—

SHARON: From his mouth.

FARSTED: Trophy necklace.

SHARON: What?

FARSTED: His trophy necklace.

SHARON: Whose?

FARSTED: My father was a hero.

(*Pause*)

SETH: With a hero's decorations.

FARSTED: They were all put away.

SHARON: Why didn't you turn them in, report them—

FARSTED: They weren't doing any harm. You call somebody official, you tell them you've got bombs, you're in trouble. Sir, my Daddy was a hero.

SETH: Could your son have been hoping to learn how his grandfather could be a hero and do terrible things like this?

FARSTED: This...I always thought there was a warrior's code. Soldiers from both sides did it. Always have.

SHARON: Madness. Insanity.

SETH: People drive themselves insane when they feel it's expected of them. So they can do our terrible things. Could that be why your son brought them to Show and Tell? So he could learn how to feel about it?

FARSTED: Feel about what?

SETH: That he was on this earth thanks to atrocities. His grandfather survived and had you, and you had him. How could he be a fair exchange for all those people's blood? Maybe he wanted to know.

FARSTED: He was nine years old.

SETH: I want to know. Don't you?

FARSTED: I don't dwell on it.

SETH: We all dwell on it. It is the question we dwell on. I wonder how long ago he found that footlocker. I wonder how long he waited to find someone—someone like Corey—who might help him understand what it meant. (*Beat*) Mister Farsted, we'll be turning our findings over to the governor. You'd better prepare your family.

FARSTED: If I could—is there any chance of getting my son, at this time?

SETH: I'm afraid not.

FARSTED: I don't see why you have to keep punishing him, Sir, I don't see why you can't just let me take him home.

SETH: Mister Farsted—

FARSTED: Or it's because of these ears, I guess, but listen, you know all about remains, I didn't know who to *start* to ask before, but if you told me what I should do, what would be proper and fitting, I would do it right now.

SETH: Mister Farsted—

FARSTED: I guess people's little children get blown up all the time now. But these ears from a half-century-ago soldiers, that's really bad, I guess. But when you inherit a house, you know, all paid, decent furniture, stuff you grew up with, all belongs to you, one little footlocker, way back in the basement, everything else is good, nice town. Show me one person who would drive away and leave that. Some people would of called up the officials and said, "Look at this bad thing my Daddy had." Some people would of sold that house, tried to leave that footlocker behind for somebody else maybe. Some people aren't conscientious at all.

IRIS: Mister Farsted, we would give you your son if we could. I couldn't find him. The cause of an event this extreme tends almost to vanish. He was probably holding up a landmine to show everyone. There's nothing left. Mister Farsted, I looked and looked.

SETH: No one blames your boy. Every child goes down to a basement and opens a box and thinks he's finally found the secret that everyone is keeping. What Tommy did, one way or another, everyone does. We couldn't find him, but we recognize him. We'd know him anywhere. You may return to your home, Mister Farsted.

(FARSTED *exits.*)

SHARON: I get too angry. I take too much out on them.

IRIS: Mr Farsted kept some objects connected with death. I don't think the three of us are in a position to condemn him.

SETH: I should go see Corey.

(ANN *enters.*)

SETH: Ann, good, assemble the press.

ANN: They've all gone. I came to tell you.

SETH: No. Oh, no.

ANN: An air disaster. Hundreds of casualties. Passengers and onlookers.

SHARON: How did it happen?

ANN: All they know is hundreds of holiday travelers caught fire and fell from the sky.

IRIS: Hundreds? Two? Five?

ANN: Closer to five, I think.

IRIS: Terrible.

SHARON: Senseless tragedy.

ANN: That's what I came in to tell you, a call came from the Capitol. We have to catch a plane straight there.

SHARON: We'll have to write the report on this one on the way.

IRIS: Hundreds. Closer to five. And a name to learn for every one. Off we go.

SETH: I need to see if Corey's okay, I owe her an—

SHARON: Seth. People must be grieving by the thousand.

(*They exit as the lights fade.*)

Scene Six

(COREY *enters. She glances downstage.*)

COREY: Hi, what's the matter? (*She crouches as if to speak to a child at a little distance away, down front.*) What happened to you? Show me? Hm. Can you stop crying? Okay, you cry a little longer, then. Uh-huh? You'll have a handsome scab, there. You'll be able to pick at that for a couple of weeks. Sure you can pick at it. You should only do it if you want to get a scar, though. You could get a tough-looking scar out of that. Hey, you stopped crying, did you notice? Yeah, you'll live.

(SETH *enters.*)

SETH: Corey?

(COREY *stands.*)

SETH: Corey, Jesus, I'm glad to see you. They said you'd be here, but—I was afraid you might disappear again. You really disappeared, you know? You wouldn't believe how many people I've had out looking for you.

COREY: Seth. You didn't have to do that.

SETH: I only wanted to be sure you were all right—

COREY: I'm all right. I'm functioning. There's nothing more you have to do.

SETH: The second we finished, they took and threw me into this—it went on for miles, it was a whole landscape of—my work. I kept trying to get away to find you, and when I finally did, you were gone.

COREY: You're going to get me in trouble, someone from the government showing up asking questions. It's my first day here, I'm nervous enough as it is.

SETH: Listen. This may seem like a strange question, but.... Would you consider coming with us? You don't have to do anything, if you don't want to. Just be there. We can travel around the state together. I'll take you to all the worst places.

COREY: Seth. I'm a teacher.

SETH: You could work with the survivors if you wanted to. Find the exceptional ones, and teach them. Teach them how to look at things.

COREY: Seth...

SETH: Right. Stupid idea. I just thought.... Corey, people like us are hard to find. You'll find it gets lonely, out here. It would be good to be...adjacent to someone.

COREY: They can't find anyone who's willing to teach here. I think they barely checked my background, they were so happy to have me. They said, you don't want to work in this school, we have to warn you, it's dangerous here. (*She laughs softly.*)

SETH: May I ask you a question?

COREY: Of course.

SETH: You got out. You walked away.

COREY: What's your question?

SETH: How?

COREY: I learned so much that day. It nearly killed me. And the next day I learned something else. And I about left myself for dead. But another day came, and I picked up another fact or two. And how I come to be here is, I could not stop learning. Live people learn. So I'm here.

SETH: You're right. I learn something every day. But you know? Day after day I learn the same damn thing.

(*A school bell rings.*)

COREY: I have to go. My class will be waiting for me.

SETH: I'm glad I got to see...that you're here. I'm grateful.

COREY: So am I.

(SETH *exits.* COREY *watches him out of sight. She crosses downstage and claps her hands.*)

COREY: Class. Good morning, class. My name is Corey, and I'll be your substitute. Could someone open up those curtains, please? You and you, thank you. Let's have some sunlight here. (*The light brightens. Her eye is caught by something at slightly above eye height, downstage. Her eyes widen, but she goes on.*) Now I'll need you to tell me how far along in your texts you are. But first things first. (*She crosses behind the table, and picks up an autoharp case. She holds it briefly, and places it on the table. She looks up again.*) I always like to start with music. And so... (*She opens the case and gently lifts out an autoharp.*) This is an autoharp. It's not a fancy musical instrument. It sounds pretty lonely unless it's helping someone sing. (*She looks up again.*) Please excuse me, it's just that it's my first day, and I came up from another direction, so I didn't know. Who can tell all of us what that is? That white...building. That's right. That's the Capitol building. I had no idea it was so close. Well. Let's sing a song. I'm sure you know it, so I'll go through it for you and you join me when you're ready. (*As she plays the chords, she looks up.*) Think about all the important people sitting up there, working so hard, trying to keep things orderly. Don't you think they ought to hear you sing? They'll look up from their work and say, "Who is making all that beautiful noise?" (*Singing*)
Crying cockles and mussels
Alive, alive oh
Alive, alive oh
Alive, alive oh

Crying cockles and mussels,
Alive, alive oh...

(The lights fade.)

END OF PLAY